Along A Country Road

Bonnie DeHart

ISBN-10: 0692967605
ISBN-13: 978-0692967607

DEDICATION

This book is dedicated to Claire Swanson Bonnell, my fifth grade teacher and life-long friend, whose encouragement so many years ago, showed me the joy of writing and gave me the confidence to do so.

CONTENTS

ACKNOWLEDGMENTS

Thank you, Tony Sexton, for tenaciously leading our writers group, and providing continuous encouragement and support.

TJ Schweers, Ruth Rogers and Tony (of the original Nomadic Ink group) for your honest critiques and encouragement.

Judy Hall, Marilyn Eaton, Helen Webre for your editing expertise. Thank you Judy for your constant enthusiasm which edged me on.

Pat Williams for printing my poems in the "Forkland Community Center News" and encouraging further publication.

All my neighbors and friends along this country road who inspired this work.

INTRODUCTION – ALONG A COUNTRY ROAD:

IMPRESSIONS OF LIFE

My life, I find, is one of contrasts. I come to my country road in Kentucky from Denver, Colorado. And so, I enjoy the contrast of city vs. country life. My first impression upon arrival in this peace filled country place, indeed what brought me here, is its beauty. In contrast to semi-arid Denver, it is lush, green, so overflowing with plant life that it sometimes has to be bush hogged back just to keep my home from going under. I believe in the rains of spring and early summer, I can almost see the grass grow – minute by minute. I worry that I will not be able to keep up with it all. And I realize that is a city dweller's worry, because one of my most lingering impressions is there is a rhythm to life in the country. It takes in seasons, and surprises – storms and droughts, and knows somehow life continues through it all. There is a patience about life along a country road. A time for each task: A time to wait and a time to know when action must be taken.

My small slice of Kentucky is a place where people want to spend their lives. More than any place I've lived, I find people who have lived and worked the land here their entire lives with no thought of leaving. It is home to many not for years alone, but for generations.

Yet, life along this country road is far from easy. I have come to admire the people. It is a place rich in history and tradition. I watch as my neighbors work their land: plowing, planting, harvesting. I've seen some good harvests and years when rains washed out the crops or drought destroyed them. I watch as they cut and bale hay in the sweltering heat and humidity of long dusty hours until the job is done. I watch as their equipment breaks down midway through the job, and again, they work until the repairs are done. I marvel at their endurance, their stamina. I don't pretend to understand all the work involved. I know I have not worked as hard, as long, or as tirelessly in my lifetime.

People along my country road are self-reliant. Many of the men can repair or build just about anything. I watch them repair heavy farm equipment and make household maintenance look easy by comparison. I see families who can and preserve food from their gardens and fruit trees to carry them through the winters. Men hunt and fish to supplement their food supply. My small piece of Kentucky is not that far from its pioneer history. There is a pride and honesty in the hard work and diligence of its people.

Some work in town, leaving in the early morning darkness to get to their jobs, none close to home. Others work right here on the farms along my country road. I watch snow plows in winter, and men trimming the roadside growth of weeds and overhanging branches at least twice each summer. I can count on their arrival and enjoy the openness when they depart. Trees get trimmed; roads and utility wires repaired. When rains wash driveways' rocks and debris onto roads, neighbors take care to clear the way. I sometimes wait for the mailman who serves as "watchman" of our road – helping to resolve or report anything he sees amiss as he makes his daily rounds. I can count on a wave and a smile.

Even my weekly drive to the local recycling facility adds to the work and rhythm of this place. I can pause there a while and chat with the caretaker, catch up on the local news.

This is a place that doesn't wait for repairmen. People take it on themselves to keep things going. Neighbors help neighbors. I've learned to check at the nearest gas station/deli for help when I need it rather than using the yellow pages or internet (another city dweller's mode).

And sometimes I do have to wait. After a storm comes healing. After summer, comes fall. After a drought, eventually comes rain. Life continues, digs out, rebuilds, considers what can be done differently, moves on. I watch as farmers move cattle from field to field, separate calves from adults, work to immunize and keep healthy their investments, bring cattle to market. I watch as they plow muddy, hoof pocked fields and give them rest to grow enough to help sustain the herd again. I watch them bring hay when the weather proves again that we are small in the sight and force of nature. I can only imagine the financial struggles that accompany these tasks, since loans must be gotten to buy extra hay or carry a family through difficult times.

I have come to truly respect the depth of talent that emerges from homes and people here along my country road. There is a community of artists who work in wood, paint, metal; who work with plants and paper, feathers and flowers. I've learned Kentucky supports its artists and writers in a way I've not seen elsewhere.

The lessons of my country road are not just from observing people. There is a rhythm to nature that mimics the lives of men, or perhaps vice versa. I can sit on my porch in the quiet early morning hours and listen to the wakening day. First the whip-poor-will. I can count on their call at summer's dawn and dusk, as much as I count on the fire flies and frog song. Sometimes I hear the great horned owl, its voice echoing eerily from deep within the knobs. As the day begins I love the sound of donkey's braying, roosters crowing, cattle mooing along with the barks of dogs in the early morning hours - crows, songbirds and the pounding of woodpeckers at work on the trees. Of all the birdlife along my country road, I count my favorite feathered friend (for friends they become indeed) to be the fat little Yellow Breasted Chat, the most aptly named of all the songbirds. For chat he does from early morning throughout the day. He's easily found flapping his wings as he so un-gracefully moves from tree to tree, pausing to chit and to chat at each stopping place and to display his bright yellow breast. I smile and sometimes laugh at this wonderful happy clown of a bird. My heart leaps in joy at the sweet, sweet song of the Carolina Wren who at times graces my porch swing and sings from the depth of its being.

I watch deer and wild turkey graze through my fields. I'm angered at the havoc raccoons play on bird feeders but laugh at the docile possums who also share this land.

Each day along my country road brings reassuring sights and sounds. I enjoy the rhythm of the seasons, and I enter my observations on the pages that follow. . . Along A Country Road.

EARLY SPRING

Early spring is light and airy
compared to the density of summer.
There is a lacey, open space
between the branches of a Redbud tree in bloom.

Colors are more subtle in spring
compared to the riot of autumn hues:
Pale greens and reds of budding trees
sparkle in the sunlight,
in contrast to the grays and browns
of barren trees, which stand
tall and silent in the knobs.

Flowers are more delicate and tentative
in early spring,
compared to the hardy hosts of summer:
Dogwood and Forsythia;
Purple Violets in my lawn.
Spring Beauties, Trout Lily, and Phlox
are all but hiding among leaves and rocks.

SPRING MARCHES ON

Even though I've been watching
as each layer of spring arrives,
I'm surprised:
Leaves are dense in the knobs this morning.
Mist is rising from the hollers.
Overnight, the leaves are fully here.

Spring's lacey airiness is gone.
I've learned to savor
its transient beauty;
to enjoy, and applaud
as the show marches on.

DAFFODILS

Daffodils in full bloom,
are one day standing tall;
reaching for the sun.
The next, battered down by wind,
        and rain,
                and cold.
Only to stand again through this fickle spring.

I have a warming fire in
my woodstove this morning.

Wood-smoke and daffodils
define Kentucky's spring.

YELLOW TROUT LILY

It was by chance I found you
as I walked along my country road,
near the stream raging after yesterday's storm.

I would have passed you by,
had a speeding car not forced me to the roadside.

It was by chance I found you
in all your short-lived glory:
green, mottled leaves
and yellow flower.
It was the yellow, 'midst the rotting leaves and wood,
that caught my eye.

Beside the stream,
where few will ever see you –
You enriched my life.
You added beauty to the springtime,
And,
Sadly,
Tomorrow you'll be gone.

CHANGE OF WEATHER

Today is
Misty,
Rainy,
Cold,
Socked-in
Grey.

A total change from yesterday.

APRIL

April's gotten itself confused with March.
It came in like a lion.

    Wind

        Rain

           Sleet

              Snow

Just flurries, but they really had no right to be here
when the spring buds and new growth were only just begun.

All confused now.
Topsy-turvy.

We'll see what comes to light this year,
Since April's gotten itself confused with March.

TORNADO WARNING

Grey-green, black, heavy clouds
   Threatening
Sharp blades of lightning
   Stabbing
Sheets of Rain
   Gushing

Creating raging creeks
where none existed just moments ago.

  Wind

  Sirens

  Warnings

All visibility gone.
All safety gone.
Now here,
and as suddenly,

  Done.

Violent change.
A rift in the universe?
Global warming?

Or normal cleansing of Kentucky spring?

MAY

That which was seen
is now unseen:
Dense foliage and undergrowth
absent just a month ago,
now hides nature's scars and secrets:
      Fallen trees
      Rock slides
      Caves
      Hollow logs
      Bird nests
      Deer and wild turkeys
      and the elusive warblers.

The woodlands are now mysterious.
They are
      Dark,
      Dense,
      Impenetrable.

MAY FLOWERS

Queen Ann's Lace
and Clover
a natural bouquet,
now sprinkled with Daisies.

No Garden Club needed
to form this array.

THE CLEANSING

Limestone-lined streambeds
lie dry as a bone.
Walked on by deer seeking water in vain.

Then rain . . .
Torrential

taking with it the debris of winter.
quenching thirst.

DAWN

There is a single moment
of pure clarity
between the darkness and the dawn,
when the earth stands in silent
silhouette against the sky.
        Then
          Slowly,
          Softly,
Shadows give way to light.
Silence gives way to birdsong.
A black and white world
          Transforms:
First purples and grays.
then pinks;
sometimes vibrant oranges.

The silence is broken
by the raucous new day.

…. AND SUNSET

The same colors as sunrise
but darkening.
My mind is filled with the chatter of the day.
Only with darkness
does silence return.

.... AND AGAIN, DAWN

I try to capture the dawn with words,
but it changes before the description is right.
Instead of trying to capture it,
I should sing to it
as the birds do.

ROOTS AND VINES

Roots and vines
Anchors and skyhooks

Roots
     Stabilize
     Nourish
     Maintain
even when trees live on the
edge of a precipice.

Vines
     hold trees up
even when roots are
nearly gone and trees are
too weak to stand on their own.

Vines
     provide highways for squirrels
     and perches for birds.

Roots and vines
anchors and skyhooks -
Nature's support system.

Maybe we all need roots and vines.

MISTY SUNRISE

In the eerie mist of sunrise
I watch the white hot orb
rise over the eastern hills.
Brightening the mist,
Clarifying the landscape,
Making visible the trees,
Creating sparkling jewels of morning dew
in the spider webs dotting the fields.

The mist lingers –
stubbornly refusing to leave
as the sun rises.

The near landscape becomes clear as
the distant remains shrouded.
My neighbor's barn across the road
cannot be seen.
Mist shelters deer and wild turkeys.

I hear
birdsong,
the knocking/pounding/beating sound
of woodpecker on ancient trees.
A cow moos,
donkeys bray,
dogs bark,
all welcoming the dawn.

I mainly hear, not see, this new day.

MORNING SKY

Sliver of moon in the eastern sky,
Sharing space with the rising sun.

Sun now wins the day.
Moonlight fades away.

Buzzards lift off to share the morning sky.

FIVE A.M.

The world lies shrouded
in absolute silence.
No sound,
No movement,
Not even a breeze.
The shrill, sharp, shouts of tree frogs
raucous at days end,
now silent.
Resting.
A renewal of strength and life.
Stars are brilliant in the morning sky.
Trees black silhouettes against grey horizon.

Soon,
The great horned owl will break the quiet stillness.
Hoot – Hoot – To Hooooo...
its ghostly call,
followed by its mate's reply
from somewhere deep within the knobs.

Soon the birdsong.

Soon the dawn.

COYOTE

Coyotes appear –
heads rising above the tall hay:

watching
waiting

Before they see me and run away.

At night, I hear them:

howling
yipping

in celebration of a kill.

I am glad my dog and I are tucked safely inside.

BUZZARDS

Buzzards –
nature's cleanup crew.

Enough said.
They clean up the dead.

TURKEY DANCE

I looked out my window this morning
to see three male turkeys
strutting their stuff
right in the middle of my country road,
while eight females grazed in the field nearby.

They stood,
circled one another,
Chests puffed out,
tail feathers in full fan.

One of them apparently "won".
He strutted into the field with the females,
while the other two drifted into the woods.

I don't understand the rules of this dance.
I imagine the ornithologists do.
But I did enjoy watching the show!

GREAT BLUE

The Great Blue Heron
rose
silently through the morning mist,
glided
on broad, outspread wings
to its next site along the roadside stream.

Silently it stood
on tall stick legs,
patiently
waiting.

Head and neck plunged!
Faster than my brain could record its movement.
It grabbed a small fish in its needle sharp beak
and swallowed.

Satisfied
at rest,
the graceful bird stood among the reeds
on one leg.
Asleep?
Or continuing the hunt?
I could not tell.

Majestic,
Patient,
Quiet.

The Great Blue.

FAST AND FREE

Minnows running small rapids
darting in schools within deeper waters
swimming fast and free.

What happens when the stream runs dry?
When floods take the stream beyond its bounds?

I think they die.

It would seem the length of life
is not the important thing –
but swimming fast and free!

EARLY SUMMER RAIN

Summer rain
refreshes
causes havoc
delays the cutting and baling of hay
Yet gives life to a barren earth.

CONTROL

It's cloudy today.
It would be different
if I had my say.

CLARITY

I lie awake listening
to the silence
in the darkness

All is peaceful.

I find clarity in silence.

WIND

Where does the wind go?
I wake to wonderful breezes
and stand outside to receive its
cool refreshment.

And then,
it's gone.
The air grows dense and muggy.

Where does the wind go?
Does it move on to share its gifts with others?
Or does it simply end,
to start up again in the early morning hours?

THE OTHER FACE OF WIND

Terrible at times –
Twisting healthy trees to the ground.
Ripping roofs off homes and barns.
Blowing chairs right off my porch.

Blowing,
              Blasting,
Bending.

Powerful and Angry.
Not the gentle kite-flying kind.

EARLY JUNE

How sweet the scent of new cut hay
in the early morning dew.
Waiting for the baler
in the heat of this summer's day.
He'll be working 'til the job is done
in the hot and muggy summer's sun.

New growth already in the fields cut first,
so quickly continuing the cycle of life.

Reassuring to these old bones.

JUNE'S DENSITY

Heaviness of summer:
Dense growth-
Plants,
Weeds,
Vines so intertwined
I cannot see where one begins
and another ends.

Impossible to keep my land clear.

Dense air –
Moist,
Heavy,
No movement in the heat of the day:
Not a bird,
Not a breeze,
Not me.

As life takes to the cool, dark woods.

SUMMER DAYS

Each day is its own creation,
conceived in pre-dawn silence,
born to a misty dawn.

Sometimes cold, wet, and ugly.
Yet always growing to fulfillment.

Birds sing.
Deer graze.
Wild Turkeys strut through the fields.
Spiders spin their webs, bejeweled in the early morning dew.

Hot afternoons turn to
cool evenings.

Each day:
Darkness to rebirth.

FOR THE BIRDS

I find Warblers among the willows
Finches along the fence row
Bluebirds resting on the telephone wire.

The Great Blue Heron lifts silently
from the stream,
while Sandpipers and Kingfishers stay to
compete for minnows.

Crows dive-bomb passing Hawks.
I wonder why the Hawks don't fight back.
They just continue about their business.

Buzzards soar out of sight, catching the
lifting air
floating peacefully above the earth.
Ever searching.

The Little Green Heron sits, pear-shaped
on tree top.

Kinglets and Vireos remain a mystery.
I know they're in the nearby woods
- unseen.
In contrast, the Cardinal stands out –
bright red, and loud!

I hear the sweet song of the Carolina Wren,
and watch the King Bird catching flies.

None make me smile as much as the fat,
Yellow Breasted Chat.

I sometimes think I own this land.
But let's face it.
It's for the birds.

RAINBOWS AND BIRDSONG

If Rainbows were music
they would be birdsongs –

A Bluebird at the highest tip of a tree
singing its heart out to the sunrise.

A Sparrow's sweet song.
The lyrical voice of the Carolina Wren.

If Rainbows were music
they would be birdsongs –

The Towhee's "Drink your tea!"
The Cardinal's sharp call,
The staccato sound of the Yellow Breasted Chat.

I'm not sure we'd include the raucous Crow,
but perhaps, the mystical silence
of the Great Blue Heron in flight.

If Rainbows were music
they would be birdsongs.

RAINBOW PARADE

Sitting on my deck, I observe the bird parade fly by.
They do not know I'm watching.
They're busy going about their lives
as I enjoy the pageant:

Yellow
Red
Blue

Goldfinch, Cardinal, and Bluebird. Occasionally the vibrant Indigo Bunting.

Brown
Grey

Sparrow and Blue-Grey Gnatcatcher
Phoebe
Cat Bird and Carolina Wren
My lifelong friends, the Chickadees

Iridescent Green

Ruby Throated Hummingbirds buzz around my head
dive-bombing each other
while competing for the feeder's sweet nectar.

Bluebirds today seem busiest
caring for their young.
Ducking into and out of the birdhouse
I put up for them a year ago.

The male waits atop a nearby tree.
Checking in when his mate flies away for provisions.

During the passage of a year,
I watch winter birds move on,

launching the spring migration
while summer birds move in.
Rose-breasted Grosbeak passes through.
Yellow-breasted Chat settles in to stay.

Sometimes the daily parade stops.
I'm treated to a song.
Cardinals can be counted on for that
as can the little Chipping Sparrow.
The Wren sings its heart out
while perched on my porch swing.

Blue Jays are bullies.
I put up with them.

Mid-day I notice the parade mostly stops.
as I nap in the hammock on my deck.
The world is quiet until evensong.
Birds, it seems, rest also.

After the parade.

KENTUCKY SUMMER

For a few short hours
the earth stands absolutely silent.

Then midnight's stillness is broken
as darkness yields to dawn.
Whip-poor-will wails;
Songbirds herald first light,
rejoicing in sun's rising.

Dawn's activity gives way
to a sultry summer's day
filled with Cicada's steady rasp.
Birds feed quietly
or rest through the afternoon.

With darkness the night songs begin:
Tree frog,
Bull frog,
Cricket and Katydid.

With darkness the light show begins:
Fireflies flicker in field and trees
against a star-filled sky.

Again, the Whip-poor-will.
And sometimes the great horned owl
calls eerily through the night.

from . . .

AUGUST

Continuing heat of summer,
when we sweat just standing still.
And those who work outside
require more strength and will.

Through rain and heat,
Through work and sleep,
So now the year moves on.

to . . .

A RAINY AUTUMN

The winds and rain
take the leaves away
before their Fall colors can shine.

Autumn defers to winter's clime'
of barren trees
and icy breeze.

Brown, fallen leaves lie clumped together
on rain-soaked lawns.

We are deprived of their joyous flight:
crimson, canary, flaming oranges
gold, ruby and apricot
floating through blue skies on warm winds.

SEPTEMBER

Second cutting of hay is done.
The march to winter has begun.
Change is in the air.

A time between,
A month unsure:
Hot and humid?
A cooling chill?
Heavy early morning dew.
Dawn sleeps in;
days shorten.

And yet, summer is not through.

I hear the cattle in the morning.
Birds awaken, singing.
Crows are active;
Hummingbirds are furiously feeding,
preparing for the long trip south.
Geese fly over the land.

Stars are bright on cool, clear nights.
And still, I hear the Whip-Poor-Will.

FARMER

I don't think I have the patience
to be a farmer.
Things get done in their own time,
not mine.
Only when the weather is right does
the work begin.

I don't think I have the courage
to be a farmer.
I'd worry about the weather.
I'd trouble over it.
I would not want to wait, to hope,
to always remain ready to go.

I don't think I have the strength
to be a farmer.
I couldn't endure the summer's heat.
I don't think I could work from dawn to dark,
and beyond,
without rest –
when the weather is right and the work must be done.
Always keeping equipment ready to run.

I don't think I have what it takes
to be a farmer.
Yet, I know I would not be alive without them.

Most of us eat our potatoes and steaks,
never realizing the toll it takes.

I have come to give farmers deep respect.
They work beyond hard.
They work without rest.
Giving each season their level best.

NOVEMBER 2015

This month can't seem to make up its mind
whether to be November, or March, or even April.
70 degrees?
Really?
In Kentucky,
in November?

Purple violets are blooming in my yard,
and my azalea is budding.
What a cruel trick is being played on them this year.

Yet, I'm enjoying these beautiful days
and shoring myself up for the "real" November
which must surely be just around the corner.

Then again, when I think of it. . .
there have been a few cold days,
and some cold wind and rain.
The trees are all but leafless now.
Squirrels are actively storing food.
I see the deer, and yes, the hunters.
A sure sign that November is here.

A flock of Cedar Waxwings passed through yesterday.
The Chickadees and Juncos are active.
I already miss the songbirds of summer.
Maybe it's November after all.

I guess ol' winter's on its way –
I think I'll just enjoy this day.

HEALING

 I saw bright flashes light the evening sky at the moment I lost
electricity. Night brought bitter cold and darkness to the continuing
storm. Most of the telephone poles between my home and Rte 68 had
snapped.

The aging, lichen-covered Cherry tree had defined my Kentucky
property. It formed a boundary between my lawn and hay field. It
provided a shady sanctuary on hot summer days. It was a haven for
birds, bees and butterflies. And since the day it fell, during the ice
storm of January 2009, the huge old tree has defined my days.

I have never experienced an event as devastating as "The Ice Storm",
January 27th 2009. Neither I nor the cherry tree went down easily. It
took two cold, icy days of steady torrential rain, followed by ice, snow
and wind to fell the tree, and an additional week to make me realize
how vulnerable I was at the place I call my haven on Ward's Branch
Road in Boyle County. I'm sure Kentuckians state-wide came to similar
realizations. As I sat at my desk looking out the window that late
afternoon, silently and in slow motion, half of the great tree fell.
Overnight the second half of my Cherry Tree was downed. The huge
hulk which was my tree lay like a slain dinosaur across my lawn in the
grey, icy, foggy gloom of dawn … January 28th 2009.

As the days progressed, the eerie, light-less, ice-covered silence persisted. The only sound was that of snapping, cracking, twisting limbs and trees falling all over my property and in the surrounding knobs. None had the impact on my psyche or my land as did the old Cherry tree. Days passed. The cold persisted. Every tree, every branch, every blade of grass was covered with an inch of ice. The roads were impassable. Power lines were down and dangling from broken poles. I saw no light, no car, no human being.

Slowly, slowly I realized the storm was over and the healing had begun. The bird feeder that had hung on the cherry tree had landed upright beneath an arch of the tree's giant trunk. I crawled under the fallen tree and filled the feeder. Birds ate hungrily of the seeds. Three pair of blue birds huddled under the eaves of my garden shed each evening. I admired their tenacity and decided if they could survive the ice, so could I.

A friend brought me useable water. A neighbor whom I'd never before met (see "Alton Hall – a trilogy" in the pages that follow) offered to bring me more fire wood. He'd laughed at me, the city slicker, "You'll need a lot more wood than that," he'd said.

It was four days before Wards Branch Road was passable and two weeks before power was restored. I will not forget my first outing to Wal-Mart to find empty shelves. There was no bottled water, no kerosene or lamp oil, no generators, no candles and no batteries. Everything I normally take for granted was gone. . . a warm home, electricity, potable water.

I left Kentucky. A bluebird perched high atop a broken tree in the early morning sunshine as I drove away. I held that image. An image of hope and endurance. I will never forget seeing caravans of power trucks driving into the state as I was leaving. Heroes, I thought. Those men are heroes. It was two months before I returned to my Kentucky land and the great, fallen tree.

Through the rest of 2009, my land and I continued the gradual healing. A neighbor cut up the cherry tree and over the month of April I burned the smaller limbs, gave some of the wood to a craftsman, stacked some for firewood. The tree will live on in the cherry wood bowls and benches that will be made of it. I was again able to mow the lawn after clearing bushels of twigs. The hay fields grew; the hay was cut and baled. Blue birds nested and raised their young.

Most of the scars from the storm were not noticeable under the thick foliage of summer. I had more trees trimmed in the fall. Not until winter were the damaged tree limbs which had twisted, snapped and broken again a visible reminder of what had been. There was more work to be done to clean up the land. Yet I know now time and effort will take care of it. I've now read that churches were giving out warm meals, and the National Guard was not far from my place handing out generators to critical sites such as nursing homes. But I had no news during the storm. I felt isolated and alone. I know now that I can survive and that nature takes its course to live and to thrive. I know now what I need to be better off should another storm hit central Kentucky: a generator, radio, candles, matches, wood for my woodstove, water, easily prepared food and something to cook it on.

I know help comes, ice melts, power is restored.

Only the stump of the cherry tree remains now in my lawn. I'll put a bird feeder on it. Perhaps I'll plant some flowers around it as a reminder of what was and of what can be - a reminder of survival and healing. It is a reminder of the hard work and endurance of Kentuckians – a reminder that heroes come in many guises: neighbors, friends and men who work for power companies.

IN MEMORY OF ALTON HALL

A TRILOGY

PART I: STARTLED

My dog barked at the flashing lights
across the road.
Ambulance.

I watched the flashing lights
in the darkness
and the rain.

The ambulance left
quietly.

I think my neighbor died last night
Alone.

I watched the world return to darkness
when the ambulance drove off.

Change is coming to my country road.

PART II: CHANGE

The world's a little emptier today.
Alton Hall, who has lived along our country road
his entire life,

Has died.

I saw him only last week on his tractor,
readying a patch of land for planting.

I'll miss him.

We'd always wave when both outside,
and catch up on the local news
when picking up our mail from the boxes
at the end of our driveways,
where only the narrow road separated our lands.

We'd help each other,
and watch out for each other.

The world's a little emptier today.
A man who has lived along our country road
his entire life

Has died.

His farm sits silent today.
Leaving the universe forever changed.

PART III: NEVER THE SAME AGAIN

Alton Hall has died
Everything looks the same as always this morning
along our country road.
Sun rose as always
bringing light to the serenity of night.
Redbud, Forsythia in full bloom contrasted
against the vibrant green grass.
Dogwood blossoms about to pop open.
Buzzards lifting off toward the skies to start
their daily hunt.
Crows are cawing; Cardinals sing.
Everything looks the same as always this morning
along our country road.

But

It is not the same and never will be again.

Alton Hall has died.

His land across from mine will never feel his hand again
will never know his care.
A lifetime of planting and harvest,
a family raised;
This country road will never feel his footsteps again.

Alton Hall has died and yesterday was buried
just a mile from his home.
That seems fitting.
He is a part of this place
now forever.

And change has come to our country road.

MISTY MORNING

The earth slept in this morning
in silence,
under a heavy mist that smothered the sun's rising.
Spiders slept in their dew-covered webs.
Deer grazed, across the fields at tree line,
shrouded in the mist.

Hours elapsed, as the push and pull
of mist against sunrise
played out its ritual tug of war.

Slowly,
Slowly,
sun won the struggle.
The earth awoke to a bright new day!

GIVING BACK

As long as I've lived in my place
along the country road,
the old dead tree has stood
at the curve near the top of the hill.

Limb-less.

Home to raccoons,
Fodder for Woodpeckers.

As steadfastly as it has stood,
So graciously it fell
in last night's storm.
Into the woods,
away from the road
causing no concern for passers-by.
I barely noticed.

Its life now finds completion in returning to the land.
Its final gift –
to rebuild the soil.
And yet, for just a while longer,
lying flat now on the ground –
it remains a home for small bugs and critters,
and fodder for Woodpeckers.

NEIGHBORS

Is it that there are fewer people here
along my country road than in the city,
such that each is better known?

Or

Is it that we depend on each other,
watch out for each other,
help each other,
reveal more of each other in our common needs
along my country road?

LIFE

It's easy to feel the cycle of life
in the country.
The icy chill of Winter
gives way to the gentle growth of Spring.
Red Bud and Dogwood and delicate wild flowers
are followed by Summer's hot, muggy, density
and fall's cooling colors.

Preparing, planting,
harvest; rest –
the cycle of life.

Birth, growth,
maturity; death.
Rebirth, renewal –
the cycle of life.

W. G. COOLEY
        August 1, 2017

W.G. Cooley died today.

His land lies fallow
anticipating change.

The keepers of history
along this country road
are moving on.

IMPRESSIONS

In the city
I rush from meeting to meeting.
I drive from place to place,
consumed by life's noise and busy-ness.

In the country
I find a rhythm that
considers the seasons of the year,
and the extremes within those seasons:
Flood and drought,
Snow and ice,
Heat and cold.

The unrelenting heat and humidity of August
gives way to Autumn's vibrance,
moves on to Winter's bone-chilling cold,
and to the extremities of Spring –
Gentle growth of wild flowers;
violent floods.

In the stillness before dawn, I find a quiet
that gives respite to my soul.

It takes in the season and surprises,
yet knows that life continues through it all:
Storm and drought,
Sunshine and rain,
Snow and ice,
Heat and cold.

Drought: grass literally cracks under my step.
Torrential rain: my lower field becomes a raging stream.
Ice storm: no electricity for 15 days,
bitter cold weather.
A half inch of ice encases each blade of grass, each tree limb, each leaf
Walking is life threatening, driving impossible.
Landscape bears the scars of fallen trees: A changed horizon.
Mudslides close my country road Derby Day 2010.

In the city everything is nearby and convenient.
The country demands more independence and skill,
More planning and will,
And
is refreshing to my soul.

MEDITATION ALONG A COUNTRY ROAD

And so, I leave you with these rambling observations along my country road:

I walk with my dog, Abby Rose, along my country road each day. At most, two cars may pass our way. Generally the road is ours alone, quiet and peaceful in the early morning coolness, or near sunset. I have come to realize walking is my chosen form of meditation. My mind relaxes into the rhythm of each step, internal chatter stops and I begin to see, as if for the first time, the beauty and life around me. I focus on my surroundings. I relax. I inevitably become thankful ... thankful for another day. Thankful for the silent beauty. Thankful for the sun, or mist, or rain – whatever is the menu of the day. Thankful for the flowers of springtime, the vibrant green of summer, colors of the leaves of autumn, and yes, thankful for the cold, damp barrenness of winter. I will admit that the rain, if anything but gentle, keeps me at home. Yet, walking as I do each day, I have come to appreciate the variety of each experience. I lose myself. I am more flexible after my walk than before. I do not hold as fiercely to my own agenda. I have been in the presence, you see, of something much larger, and more alive than merely me.

I walk the same two mile stretch of country road each day, day in and day out, come what may. You might think that boring. I find it anything but. My neighbors may think me crazy. I don't know. I'm afraid to ask what they think. I'm content with the knowledge that most of them wave to me as we pass. I find each day, each walk, a totally unique experience. What doesn't change is that as I walk, I relax, and as I relax, I appreciate all that I am, all that I have, and all that I have experienced.

My country road is narrow. If two cars meet, one has to pull off the road to let the other pass. Abby Rose and I have to be careful, watchful ... ready to dive into the meadow or woods on the shoulder of the road should a car or pickup come by too quickly. I like to think I've slowed the traffic as the local residents are getting used to seeing me and my dog. They seem to take the curves more slowly than they used to, anticipating that we might be there. Many will stop and share the local news for a few minutes before they continue on their way. Still, there is the occasional stranger, taking the curves too quickly, never expecting to see a woman and dog in the middle of our isolated road ... never expecting to see anyone or anything. Just speeding on their way, missing out on the day.

In springtime I enjoy new beginnings. The first fuzz of new growth on trees. The wild flowers along the roadside. The spring peepers. I notice the migration of song birds. Nuthatch and Chickadees abounding in winter, are slowly joined by bluebird and bunting, and my favorite Yellow-Breasted Chat. I still can't identify most of the warblers that arrive, but rejoice when I see the Carolina Wren. As I walk past a wooded area I am occasionally gifted with the sight of the Pileated Woodpecker. It seems ancient/dinosaurish to me. I am intrigued by this shy giant. Privileged to catch a glimpse of it. When I am truly lucky I can stand and watch as it pounds a hole in a dead tree, foraging for food, or building a nest. Mostly they fly as soon as they catch sight of me. The Great Blue Heron sometimes startles me when it flies up majestically from the roadside stream a few feet ahead to its next fishing hole.

In the summertime the roadside becomes a jungle of weeds, vines and grasses. Willow trees grow along the stream. There is no breaking through the tangle of growth. I catch glimpses of the stream, houses or barns that stand out in springtime, now hidden from sight. My views are limited. I enjoy meadows and hillsides where deer and wild turkey graze and the Bob White loudly calls.

The colors of fall lead to icy roads in winter, at times limiting my walks and certainly limiting travel. I walk cautiously during hunting season; gunshots frighten Abby Rose. Winter slows me down, and slows the rhythm of life along my country road.

The earth waits for renewal.

As does my meditation
and life . . .

Along A Country Road.

PEACE

There's something quiet
in a candle
casting shadows
through the darkness.
Something soft.
Something soothing.

Be at peace.

ABOUT THE AUTHOR

Bonnie DeHart, holds Master Degrees in Social Work and Public Administration from the University of Denver. She splits her time between Denver, Colorado and Gravel Switch, Kentucky, site of this particular country road. Throughout her career in county government, Bonnie has done grant and public regulation writing. Now in retirement, she enjoys the creativity of writing poetry. Bonnie has completed writing courses from the Longridge Writers Group, has been published in local newspapers, and continues her writing avocation with "Along A Country Road".